PIONEER VALLEY EDUCATIONAL PRESS, INC

CLOUDS

RUTH MATTISON

Look at the sky.
Can you see
any clouds up there?
A cloud is made
of many **drops**
of water or ice.

The air is filled
with water from the ground.
You cannot see the water
in the air.
The water in the air
is a **vapor**.

Clouds are made when the vapor goes up to where the air is very cold.

Clouds look white because they **reflect** the light of the sun.

Clouds look gray
when they become so thick
that you cannot see
the sunlight.

Can you see clouds
moving in the sky?
Wind moves the clouds.
Sometimes a cloud is moving
at more than
100 miles per hour.

Some clouds are
low in the sky,
and some clouds are
very high up
in the sky.

Look at the many kinds of clouds you can see in the sky.

cirrus

cumulonimbus

stratus

cumulus

drops

a very small amount
of liquid

reflect

to throw back light

vapor

a mist or a gas